The Twelve

(Translator: Paul R. Coleman-Norton)

Alpha Editions

This edition published in 2024

ISBN : 9789362513779

Design and Setting By
Alpha Editions
www.alphaedis.com
Email - info@alphaedis.com

Contents

INTRODUCTION

The legal history of Rome begins properly with the Twelve Tables. It is strictly the first and the only Roman code,[1] collecting the earliest known laws of the Roman people and forming the foundation of the whole fabric of Roman Law. Its importance lies in the fact that by its promulgation was substituted for an unwritten usage, of which the knowledge had been confined to some citizens of the community, a public and written body of laws, which were easily accessible to and strictly binding on all citizens of Rome.

Till the close of the republican period (509 B.C.-27 B.C.) the Twelve Tables were regarded as a great legal charter. The historian Livy (59 B.C.-A.D. 17) records: "Even in the present immense mass of legislation, where laws are piled on laws, the Twelve Tables still form the fount of all public and private jurisprudence."[2]

This celebrated code, after its compilation by a commission of ten men (*decemviri*), who composed in 451 B.C. ten sections and two sections in 450 B.C., and after its ratification by the (then) principal assembly (*comitia centuriata*) of the State in 449 B.C., was engraved on twelve bronze[3] tablets (whence the name Twelve Tables), which were attached to the Rostra before the Curia in the Forum of Rome. Though this important witness of the national progress probably was destroyed during the Gallic occupation of Rome in 387 B.C., yet copies must have been extant, since Cicero (106 B.C.-43 B.C.) says that in his boyhood schoolboys memorized these laws "as a required formula."[4] However, now no part of the Twelve Tables either in its original form or in its copies exists.

The surviving fragments of the Twelve Tables come from the writings of late Latin writers and fall into these four types:

(1) Fragments which seem to contain the original words (or nearly so) of a law, "modernized" in spelling and to some extent in formation;

(2) Fragments which are fused with the context of the quoter, but which otherwise exhibit little distortion;

(3) Fragments which not only are fused with the sentences of the citer but also are much distorted, although these preserve in paraphrase the purport of the provisions of a law;

(4) Passages which present only an interpretation (or an opinion based on interpretation) or a title or a convenient designation of a law.

Only in very few cases do we know or can we conjecture the number of the tablet whereon any law appeared. Consequently of the arrangement very little is ascertainable and the attribution of some items to certain tablets is debatable. The probable order of the fragments, which total over 115, has been inferred from various statements and from other indications of ancient authors.

The amount of detail apparently varies either with the importance of the matter or with the degree of general or particular knowledge of the subject supposed by the commissioners to be held commonly by the citizens. The style is characterized by such simplicity and by such brevity that the meaning in some instances borders upon obscurity,—at least so far as modern interpretation is concerned.

The value of the Twelve Tables consists not in any approach to symmetrical classification or even to terse clarity of expression, but in the publication of the method of procedure to be adopted, especially in civil cases, in the knowledge furnished to every Roman of high or low degree as to what were both his legal rights and his legal duties, in the political victory won by the plebeians, who compelled the codification and the promulgation of what had been largely customary law interpreted and administered by the patricians primarily in their own interests.

THE TWELVE TABLES[5]

TABLE I. PROCEEDINGS PRELIMINARY TO TRIAL

1. If he (the plaintiff) summon [the defendant] to court (*in ius*), he (the defendant) shall go. If he (the defendant) go not, he (the plaintiff) shall call a witness thereto. Then only he (the plaintiff) shall take [the defendant] by force.

2. If he (the defendant) attempt evasion or take to flight, he (the plaintiff) shall lay hand [on the defendant].

3. If disease or [old] age shall be an impediment, he who shall summon [the defendant] to court (*in ius*) shall grant [him] a conveyance; if he (the plaintiff) shall not wish, he (the plaintiff) shall not spread [with cushions] a covered carriage.

4. For a freeholder (taxpayer whose fortune is valued at not less than 1,500 *asses*[6]) a freeholder shall be surety (*vindex*) [for his appearance at trial]. For a proletary (non-taxpayer whose fortune is rated at less than a freeholder's) any one who shall be willing shall be surety (*vindex*).

5. When they (the parties) come to terms, [an official] shall announce [it].[7]

6. If they (the parties) agree not on terms, they shall state [their] case in the *comitium* (meeting-place) or, in the *forum* (market-place) ere noon. Both (parties) shall appear in person and shall argue the matter.

7. [If one of the parties shall not have appeared,] after noon [the judge] shall adjudge the case (*lis*) in favor of him present.

8. If both (parties) be present, sunset shall be the time-limit [of the proceedings].

9. [Both parties shall post] sureties (*vades*) and subsureties (*subvades*) [for their appearance].

TABLE II. TRIAL

1. The legal action of solemn deposit (*sacramenti actio*) [demands that each litigant shall wager either 500 *asses* or 50 *asses*]: 500 *asses* for solemn deposit (*sacramentum*) when the subject of the dispute [is valued at] 1,000 *asses* or more, 50 *asses* when [estimated at] less [than 1,000 *asses*]. [But] if the controversy concerns the liberty of a human being [, however valuable may be the person], the solemn deposit (*sacramentum*) [shall be] 50 *asses*.

2. A dangerous disease or a day appointed [for the hearing of a case] with an alien [, when the latter is a party] ... If any of these (circumstances) be an impediment for judge (*index*)[8] or arbitrator (*arbiter*)[9] or party (*reus*),[10] on this account the day of trial shall be deferred.

3. Whoever shall have need of evidence, he shall go on every third day[11] to cry[12] before the doorway [of the witness's house].

TABLE III. DEBT

1. Of debt acknowledged and for matters judged in court (*in iure*) thirty days shall be allowed by law [for payment or for satisfaction].[13]

2. After that [elapse of thirty days without payment] hand shall be laid on (*manus iniectio*) [the debtor]. He shall be brought into court (*in ius*).

3. Unless he (the debtor) discharge the debt or unless some one appear in court (*in iure*) to guarantee payment for him, he (the creditor) shall take [the debtor] with him. He shall bind [him] either with thong or with fetters, of which the weight shall be not less than fifteen pounds or shall be more, if he (the creditor) choose.

4. If he (the debtor) choose, he shall live on his own [means]. If he live not on his own [means], [the creditor,] who shall hold him in bonds, shall give [him] a pound of bread daily; if he (the creditor) shall so desire, he shall give [him] more.

5. Unless they (the debtors) make a compromise, they (the debtors) shall be held in bonds for sixty days. During those days they shall be brought to [the magistrate] into the *comitium* (meeting-place) on three successive market-days and the amount for which they have been judged liable shall be declared publicly. Moreover on the third market-day they (the debtors) shall suffer capital punishment (*capite poenae*) or shall be delivered for sale beyond the Tiber [River].

6. On the third market-day they (the creditors) shall cut pieces.[14] If they shall have cut more or less [than their shares], it shall be with impunity (*s[in]e fraude*).

TABLE IV. PATERNAL POWER

1. A dreadfully deformed child shall be killed quickly.

2. If a father thrice surrender a son for sale, the son shall be free from the father.[15]

3. [To repudiate his wife her husband] shall order her to mind her own affairs, shall take [her] keys [, shall expel her].

4. Into a legal inheritance he who has been in the womb (*in utero*) is admitted [, if he shall have been born].[16]

TABLE V. INHERITANCE AND GUARDIANSHIP

1. Women shall remain under guardianship (*tutela*), even though they shall become of full age (*perfecta aetas*)[17] ... the Vestal Virgins are excepted [and] shall be free [from control].

2. The mancipable (conveyable or movable) possessions of a woman who is under tutelage of [her] agnates[18] shall not be acquired rightfully by usucapion (long usage or long possession), save if these (possessions) by herself shall have been delivered with the sanction of [her] guardian (*tutor*).[19]

3. According as a person shall have ordered regarding his property or the guardianship (*tutela*) of his estate, so shall be the law (*ita ius esto*).

4. If a person die intestate (*intestatus*) and have no self-successor (*suus heres*), the [deceased's] nearest male agnate shall have possession of the estate.

5. If there be no male agnate, the [deceased's] clansmen[20] shall have possession of the estate.

6. To persons[21] for whom a guardian (*tutor*) shall not have been appointed by will (*testamentum*), to them [their] agnates shall be guardians.

7. If a person be insane (*furiosus*), if there be not a guardian (*custos*) for him, rightful authority over his person and over his property shall belong to [his] agnates and [in default of these] to [his] clansmen. If a person be a spendthrift (*prodigus*), he shall be prohibited from [administering his own] goods and he shall be under the guardianship (*curatio*) of [his] agnates.

8. If a freedman (*libertus*) shall have died intestate without self-successor, [his] patron (*patronus*) shall take the inheritance of a Roman citizen-freedman ... from said household into said household.

9. Items which are in the category of debts [due to or incurred by a deceased person] shall be divided [among his consuccessors] by mere operation of law (*ipso iure*) [in proportion] to [their] portions of the inheritance.[22]

10. Apportionment of an estate (*actio familiae erciscundae*) [occurs], when coheirs (*coheres*) wish to withdraw from common [and equal] participation [in the inheritance].[23]

TABLE VI. OWNERSHIP AND POSSESSION

1. When a person shall make bond (*nexum*) and conveyance (*mancipium*), according as he has specified with [his] tongue, so shall be the law (*ita ius esto*).

2. Both conveyance (*mancipatio*) and surrender in court (*in iure cessio*) are confirmed.

3. Articles which have been sold and delivered are not acquired by the buyer otherwise than if he has paid the price to the seller or has satisfied him in some other way, that is, by providing a guarantor (*expromissor*) or a security (*pignus*).

4. It shall be sufficient to make good those [faults] which have been named by [one's] tongue, [while] for those [flaws] which he (the vendor) has denied expressly [, when asked about these,] he (the vendor) shall undergo a penalty of double [damages].[24]

5. For a loyal person and for a person restored to allegiance there shall be the same right (*ius*) of bond (*nexum*) and of conveyance (*mancipium*) with the Roman people.[25]

6. Against an alien (*hostis*) title of ownership (*auctoritas*) shall be [valid] forever.[26]

7. A prescriptive title (*usucapio*) of movable things is completed by one year's [possession], but [a prescriptive title] of an estate and of buildings [is completed] by two years' [possession].

8. A person [who had been a slave and] who has been declared to be a free man [in a will on some condition], if he shall have given 10,000 [*asses*] to the heir, although he (the slave) has been alienated by the heir, by giving the money to the purchaser shall enter into his freedom.

9. If any woman [not married by *confarreatio*[27] or by *co-emptio*[28]] be unwilling to be subjected in this manner [by *usus* (possession)] to the hand of her husband (*in manum mariti*), she shall be absent [from his house] for three successive nights in every year and by this means shall interrupt the *usus* (possession) of each year.[29]

10. If the (the parties) join [their] hands [on the disputed property when pleading] in court (*in iure*), [the actual possessor shall retain provisional possession; but, when it is a case of personal freedom, the magistrate] shall grant the right of claim (*vindicia*) [provisionally to the party] asserting [the person's] freedom.

11. [If he find that another has used his timber (*tignum*)[30] in building a house or in supporting vines,] a person shall not dislodge from the framework the

timber fixed in buildings in vineyard; [but he shall have the right of action] for double [damages] against him who has been convicted of fixing [such timber].

12. Whenever [the vines] have been pruned, until fruit shall have been gathered [therefrom, the owner shall not recover the timber].

TABLE VII. REAL PROPERTY

1. [Ownership] within [a strip of] five feet [along a boundary] shall not be acquired by long usage (*usucapio*).[31]

2. The way round [each outer wall of a building] shall be two and one-half feet.

3. If they (the parties) disagree, boundaries shall be marked by three arbitrators (*arbiter*).[32]

4. [Regulations relating to] inclosures, inherited plots, cottages.[33]

5. The width of a road [extends to] eight feet on a straight [stretch], [but it extends to] sixteen [feet] on a bend.

6. [Neighboring] persons shall mend the roadway. If they keep it not laid with stones, one shall drive [one's] beast vehicles [across the land] where one shall wish.

7. If rain-water do damage [through artificial diversion from its natural channels, the offending owner] shall be restrained by an arbitrator (*arbiter*).

8. If a water-course directed through a public place shall do damage to a private person, to the [same] private person shall be [the right to bring] an action (*actio*), that damage shall be repaired for the owner.

9. Branches of a tree may be lopped all around to a height of fifteen feet.[34] If a tree on a neighbor's farm [be bent crooked] by the wind [and] lean over one's farm, [one can take] legal action (*agere*) for removal of that [tree or at least of the offending part of it].

10. [The owner of a tree] may gather its fruit which falls upon another's farm.

TABLE VIII. TORTS OR DELICTS

1. If any person had sung or had composed a song,[35] which caused slander[36] or insult to another person ... he should be clubbed to death.[37]

2. A person who had sung an evil spell ... [38]

3. If a person has broken another's limb (*membrum*),[39] unless he make agreement [for compensation] with him, there shall be retaliation in kind (*talio*).[40]

4. If a person has broken or has bruised a bone with hand club, he [shall] undergo a penalty of 300 [*asses*, if] to [an injured] freeman, [or] of 150 [*asses*,] if to [an injured] slave.

5. If a person shall have done [simple] harm (*iniuria*) to another, penalties shall be 25 *asses*.

6. [If] a person shall have caused loss ... [41]

7. If a quadruped shall be said to have caused damage (*pauperies*), legal action (*actio*) [shall be sanctioned] either for the surrender of the thing which made the damage[42] or for the offer of assessment for the damage.

8. [If a person] pasture [his] cattle [on a neighbor's land, he shall be liable to a legal action].[43]

9. He who has enchanted crops[44] ... nor should he decoy another's corn ... [45]

10. For pasturing on or for cutting secretly by night [another's] crops acquired by tillage [shall be] in the case of an adult hanging and death [by sacrifice] to Ceres;[46] a person under the age of puberty (under 15 years of age) [shall] either be scourged at the discretion [of the magistrate] or make composition by [paying] double [damages] for the harm [done].

11. Who shall have destroyed by burning a building or a stack of corn set alongside a house is ordered to be bound, scourged, burned to death, provided that knowingly and consciously he shall have committed this; but if this be by accident [, that is] by negligence, either he is ordered to repair the damage or, if he be too poor to be competent for such punishment, he shall be chastised more lightly.

12. Any person who shall have felled wrongfully (*iniuria*) other persons' trees shall pay 25 asses for every [tree].

13. If theft has been done by night, if [owner] has killed him (the thief), he (the thief) shall be [held] killed lawfully (*iure*).

14. It is forbidden that a thief be killed by day ... Unless he (the thief) defend himself with a weapon, even though he (the thief) shall have come with a weapon, unless he (the thief) shall use that weapon and shall resist, you shall not kill him. And even if he (the thief) resist, [you] shall shout [, that some persons may hear and assemble].[47]

15. In the case of all other thieves caught in the act [it is ordained] that freemen be scourged and be adjudged [as bondsmen] to the person against whom the theft has been committed, provided that they had done this by day and had not defended themselves with a weapon; that slaves caught in the act of theft be whipped with scourges and be thrown from the rock;[48] that boys below the age of puberty (under 15 years old) be flogged at [the magistrate's] discretion and that damage done by them be repaired.

16. Thefts which have been discovered through [use of] platter and loincloth [shall be punished just as if the culprits had been caught in the act]. For cases of stolen goods discovered (*furtum conceptum*) [by other means than by platter and loincloth] or introduced (*furtum oblatum*) the penalty is triple [damages].[49]

17. If a person plead on case of theft, in which [the thief] shall not be caught in the act, [the thief] shall compound for the loss by [paying] double [damages].[50]

18. A stolen thing is debarred from prescription (*usucapio*).[51]

19. No person shall practise usury at a rate of more than one-twelfth[52] ... [if he do,] a usurer shall be condemned for quadruple [damages].

20. In a suit concerning an article deposited [with a person who has failed to return the article] legal action (*actio*) for double [damages is granted].

21. [If] guardians (*tutor et curator*) [be suspected of mal-administration, there is] the right to accuse [them] on suspicion ... the legal action (*actio*) against guardians (*tutor*) [shall be] for double [damages].

22. If a patron (*patronus*) shall have defrauded a client (*cliens*), he shall be forfeited solemnly (*sacer*).[53]

23. Whoever shall have allowed himself to be called as a witness or shall have been a scales-bearer (*libripens*),[54] if he [as a witness] pronounce not his testimony, he shall be dishonored and incapable of giving evidence (*intestabilis*).

24. The penalty for false testimonies [is] that any person who has been convicted of speaking false witness [shall be] precipitated from the Tarpeian Rock.

25. If a weapon has sped from one's hand rather than [if the wielder] has hurled [it, ... he shall atone for the accidental deed by providing] the substitution of a ram [as a peace-offering to prevent blood-revenge].

26. [For administering] a noxious drug ...

27. No person shall hold nocturnal meetings in the city.

28. Members of guilds have the power to make for themselves any binding rule which they may wish, provided that they violate nothing in accordance with public law (*publica lex*).

TABLE IX. PUBLIC LAW

1. Laws of personal exception (*privilegium*)[55] shall not be proposed.

2. [Laws] concerning the person (*caput*)[56] of a citizen shall not be passed except by the greatest assembly (*maximus comitiatus*)[57] and through those whom they (the consuls)[58] have placed upon the registers of the citizenry.

3. A judge (*iudex*) or an arbitrator (*arbiter*) legally (*iure*) appointed, who has been convicted of receiving money for declaring a decision, shall be punished capitally (*capite*).

4. [Provisions pertaining to] the investigators of murder (*quaestor parricidii*) [appointed to have charge over capital cases].

5. Whoever shall have incited a public enemy (*hostis*) or whoever shall have delivered a citizen (*civis*) to a public enemy shall be punished capitally (*capite*).

6. It is forbidden to put to death ... unconvicted any one whomsoever.

TABLE X. SACRED LAW

1. A dead person shall not be buried or burned in the city.[59]

2. More than this shall not be done. The funeral pyre (*rogum*) shall not be smoothed with the axe.[60]

3. [Expenses of a funeral shall be limited to] three [mourners wearing] veils and one [mourner wearing] small purple tunic and ten flute-players.

4. Women shall not tear their cheeks or have a *lessus* (sorrowful outcry)[61] on account of the funeral.

5. The bones of a dead person shall not be collected that one may make a funeral afterward.[62] An exception is for death in battle or on foreign soil.[63]

6. Anointing by slaves and every kind of drinking-bout is abolished ... [there shall be] no costly sprinkling, no myrrh-spiced drink, no long garlands, no incense-boxes.

7. Whoever wins a crown (*corona*)[64] himself or through his chattel[65] or by his valor, [a crown] is bestowed on him [, when he is burned or buried] ... on him (who has won it) and on his father [it shall be laid] with impunity (*sine fraude*).

8. This also shall not be done: to make more than one funeral and to spread more than one bier for one person.

9. Gold shall not be added [to a corpse]. But him whose teeth shall have been fastened with gold, if a person shall bury or shall burn him with that (gold), it shall be with impunity (*sine fraude*).

10. It is forbidden for a new pyre (*rogum*) or a burning-mound (*bustum*) to be erected nearer than sixty feet to another person's buildings without the owner's consent.[66]

11. It is forbidden for a vestibule of a sepulcher (*forum*) and a burning-mound (*bustum*)[67] to be acquired by usucapion.

TABLE XI. SUPPLEMENTARY LAWS

1. Intermarriage (*conubium*) between plebeians and patricians shall not occur.[68]

2. [Regulations] concerning intercalation.

3. [Declaration concerning] days deemed favorable for official legal action (*dies agendi*).

TABLE XII. SUPPLEMENTARY LAWS

1. [There shall lie] a levy of distress (*pignoris capio*)[69] against a person who has bought an animal for sacrifice and pays not the price; likewise against a person who makes not payment for that yoke-beast which any one has lent for this purpose, that therefrom he may raise money to spend on a sacred banquet (sacrifice).

2. If a slave shall have committed theft or shall have done damage ... with his master's knowledge ... the action for damages (*actio noxalis*) is in the slave's name. Arising from delicts committed by children and by slaves of a household ... actions for damages (*actio noxalis*) shall be appointed, that the father or the master can be allowed either to undergo assessment of the suit (*litis aestimatio*) or to deliver [the delinquent] for punishment.[70]

3. If a person has taken [a thing by] a false claim,[71] if he should wish ... the magistrate shall grant three arbitrators (*arbiter*); by their [adverse] arbitration (*arbitrium*) ... [the defendant] shall compound for loss caused by [paying] double [damages from enjoyment of the article].[72]

4. It is forbidden to dedicate for consecrated use (*in sacrum*) any thing of which there is a controversy [about its ownership]; otherwise a penalty of double [the amount involved] shall be suffered.[73]

5. Whatsoever last the people have ordained, this shall be binding and valid (*ius ratumque*).[74]

UNPLACED FRAGMENTS

There are extant about a dozen fragments of whose place in the Twelve Tables we are ignorant. In nearly every instance these fragments consist of only one word or phrase, which later Latin antiquarians have preserved to illustrate an ancient spelling or to explain an archaic usage or to point a definition.

The longest fragment only is worth reproduction for the present purpose: To appeal from any judgement (*inuicium*) and sentence (*poena*) is allowed.[75]

NOTES

[1] The code was known under two titles: *Lex Duodecim Tabularum* (Law of Twelve Tables) and *Duodecim Tabulae* (Twelve Tables).

[2] *Ab Vrbe Condita*, III. 34. 6. This claim—that these statutes were the source of all public and private law—is exaggerated. Rather the code is chiefly an exposition of private law, derived from customary law, which already existed, and contains some public and religious law as well.

For another estimate see Cicero, *De Oratore*, I. 44. 195, where the advocate asserts that "the small manual of the *Twelve Tables* by itself surpasses the libraries of all the philosophers both in weight of authority and in wealth of utility."

[3] Such is the almost unanimous tradition; but one source says ivory (*eboreas*). Since some scholars scout the use of ivory in Rome at that time, the emendation of *eboreas* to *roboreas* (wooden) is suggested.

[4] *De Legibus*, II. 23. 59: *ut carmen necessarium*.

[5] Words between [ ] complete the sense of a sentence. Words between ( ) are either definitions or translations.

[6] The *as* originally was a bar (one foot in length) of *aes* (copper), then a weight, then a coin weighing one pound and worth about $.17. From time to time the *as* was reduced in weight and was depreciated in value, until by the provisions of the Lex Papiria in 191 B.C. the *as* weighed one-half ounce and was valued at $.008.

[7] Some scholars suggest that this statute should be translated thus: "When the parties agree on preliminaries, each party shall plead."

[8] The *index* hears cases in which a fixed amount is to be adjudged.

[9] The *arbiter* hears cases in which an indefinite sum is to be assessed.

[10] At this time in the language *reus* means any litigant; in later Latin *reus* is restricted to signify the defendant.

[11] Perhaps "on every other day" or "on three market-days" is meant.

[12] This means, we suppose, that the litigant requiring evidence must proclaim his need by shouting certain legal phrases before the residence of the person who is capable of supplying such evidence and who thereby is summoned to court.

[13] Some scholars suggest that the Latin represented by the words "and for matters in court" should be omitted and that the passage should open "For persons judged liable for acknowledged debt", thus restricting the period of

thirty days' grace only to matters of debt. Even if this view be correct, it disproves not the probability that the thirty days applied to various kinds of cases.

[14] "Shall cut pieces" (*partes secanto*) is explained variously: "to divide the debtor's functions or capabilities", "to claim shares in the debtor's property", "to divide the price obtained for the sale of the debtor's person", "to divide the debtor's family and goods", "to announce to the magistrate their shares of the debtor's estate"; the old Roman writers, however, understand by the phrase that the creditors can cut their several shares of the debtor's body!

[15] In primitive times a father can sell his son into slavery. If the buyer free the son, the son reënters his father's control (*patria potestas*).

Here apparently we have an old *formula* surviving in a sham triple sale, whereby a descendant is liberated from the authority of an ascendant, or after a triple transfer and a triple manumission the son is freed from his father and stands in his own right (*sui iuris*).

[16] Otherwise (an interpretation probably, perhaps not a paraphrase): "After ten months from [the father's] death a child born shall not be admitted into a legal inheritance."

[17] "Full age" for females is 25 years. For keeping women of full age under a guardian almost no reason of any worth can be urged. The common belief, that because of the levity of their disposition (*propter animi levitatem*) they often are deceived and therefore may be guided by a guardian, seems more plausible than true.

According to Roman Law of this period a woman never has legal independence: if she be not under the power (*potestas*) of her father, she is dependent on the control (*manus*) of her husband or, unmarried and fatherless, she is subject to the governance (*tutela*) of her guardian.

[18] Agnates (*agnati*) are relatives by blood or through adoption on male side only; cognates (*cognati*) are blood-relatives on either male or female side. The family of the *ius civile* is the agnatic family; the family of the *ius gentium* is the cognatic family.

[19] Beside a guardian (*tutor*) for a child of certain age (sixth statute of this Table; cf. p. 7, n. 21) there is provided also a guardian (*custos*, later *curator*) for a lunatic and for a prodigal (seventh statute of this Table).

[20] Clansmen (*gentiles*) are persons all belonging to the same clan (*gens*) as the deceased and of course include agnates, when these exist.

[21] Boys between the ages of 7 and 15, girls between the ages of 7 and 13, women neither under paternal power (*patria potestas*) nor under marital control (*in manu mariti*).

[22] Another version of this provision reads thus: "Debts bequeathed by inheritance shall be divided by automatic liability (*ipso iure*) proportionally [among the heirs], after the details shall have been investigated."

[23] That is, the judicial division of an estate by a *iudex* among the disagreeing coheirs.

[24] That is, double the proportionate part of the price or of the things transferred.

[25] This statute is set in Table I by some scholars.

[26] This probably means that a foreigner resident in Roman territory never can obtain rights over any property simply by long possession (*usu-capio*) thereof; but the meaning of *auctoritas* in this clause is disputed. At any rate *usucapio* is peculiar to Roman citizens.

This provision sometimes is placed in Table III by scholars.

[27] This is an exclusively patrician type of wedding, wherein is made a mutual offering of bread in the presence of a priest and ten witnesses.

[28] This type of wedlock, used originally by plebeians, is a fictitious sale, by which a woman is freed from either *patria potestas* or *tutela*. It comes perhaps from the primitive custom of bride-purchase.

[29] This method explains how a wife can remain married to a husband without remaining in his *manus* (rights of possession). If the *usus* be interrupted, the time of the *usus* must begin afresh, because the previous possession (*usus*) is considered as cancelled.

[30] Apparently *tignum*, as "timber" in English covers material for construction, includes every kind of material used in buildings and in vine-yards.

[31] This strip is reserved as a path between any two estates belonging to different owners. Both owners can walk on the whole space, but neither owner can claim possession of the strip through continued usage.

[32] In view of the ancient tradition that the decemvirs sent to Athens a committee to study the laws written by Solon (c. 639 B.C.—c. 559 B.C.) for the Athenians (Livy, *op. cit.*, III. 33. 5), it may not be out of place to record what Gaius (*ob. c.* 180 A.D.) reports about marking boundaries (*Digesta*, X. 1. 13): "We must remember in an action for marking boundaries (*actio finium regundorum*) that we must not overlook that old provision which was written

in a manner after the pattern of the law which at Athens Solon is said to have given. For there it is thus: 'If any man erect a rough wall alongside another man's estate, he must not overstep the boundary; if he build a massive wall, he must leave one foot to spare; a building, two feet; if he dig a trench or a hole, he must leave a space equal or about equal in breadth to depth: if a well, six feet; an olive tree or a fig tree he must plant nine feet from the other man's property and any other trees five feet.'"

While there is no evidence whatever that any enactment of the Twelve Tables reproduced in any form the terms of the Athenian statute here quoted, still the Twelve Tables may have contained some such provisions.

[33] What were these conditions we know not; all that we have from this item are the unbracketed words, which are quoted as examples of how words change their meanings and which are assigned to the Twelve Tables.

[34] Some scholars suppose that only branches over fifteen feet above ground are meant. In any case the idea is that shade from the tree may not damage a neighboring estate.

[35] We know that this item was interpreted to include prose as well as verse.

[36] Slander and libel are not distinguished from each other in Roman Law.

[37] The severity of the penalty indicates that the Romans viewed offence not as a private delict but as a breach of the public peace.

[38] Apparently an incantation against a person, for the ninth statute in this Table treats such practice against property.

[39] The penalty points to an incurable maim or break, because the next statute seems to provide for injuries which can be mended.

[40] Thus the injured person or his next of kin may maim or break limb for limb. Cf. the Mosaic *lex talionis* recorded in *Leviticus*, 24. 17-21.

[41] Most scholars connect this fragment with damage to property and conjecture that the rest of it must have been concerned with compensation for accidental damage.

[42] That is, the animal which committed the damage may be surrendered to the aggrieved person.

[43] From the context, wherein the unbracketed words are preserved, we can reconstruct the sense of this statute.

[44] Not apparently into one's own fields, but to destroy these where these were.

[45] Apparently into one's own fields by means of magical incantation.

[46] Properly the goddess of creation, occasionally (by extension) the goddess of marriage, usually the goddess of agriculture, especially the goddess of cultivation of grain and of growth of fruits in general.

Ceres is represented commonly as a matronly woman, always clad in full attire of flowing draperies, crowned either with a simple ribband or with ears of grain holding in her hand sometimes a poppy, sometimes a scepter, sometimes a sickle, sometimes a sheaf of grain, sometimes a torch, sometimes a basket full of fruits or of flowers, seated or standing in a chariot drawn by dragons or by horses.

[47] That is, the slayer must call aloud, lest he be considered a murderer trying to hide his own act.

Our sources leave it uncertain whether the law forbids that a thief be killed by day, unless he defend himself, with a weapon, or the law permits that a thief be killed, if he so defend himself.

[48] A southern spur of the Capitoline Hill, which overlooks the Forum, and named after Tarpeia, a legendary traitress, who, tempted by golden ornaments of besieging Sabines, opened to them the gate of the citadel, of which her father was a governor during the regal period. As they entered, the enemy by their shields crushed her to death: Tarpeia was buried on the Capitoline Hill, whereon stood the citadel, and her memory was preserved by the name of the Tarpeian Rock (Rupes Tarpeia), whence certain classes of condemned criminals, in later times, were thrown to their death.

[49] Our sources tell us that a person who searched for stolen property on the premises of another searched alone and naked, lest he be deemed later to have brought concealed in his clothing any article, which he might pretend then to have found in the house, save for a loincloth and a platter, on the latter of which he probably placed the stolen articles when found. We hear also that a man could institute a search in normal dress, but only in the presence of witnesses. If in the latter case stolen goods were discovered, the thief on conviction was condemned to pay thrice their value for *furtum conceptum* (detected theft). But in either case, if the accused householder could prove that a person other than himself for any reason had placed the stolen articles in his house, he could obtain from that person on conviction damages of thrice their value for *furtum oblatum* ("planted" theft). Search by platter and loincloth (*lanx et licium*) became obsolete; search with witnesses present survived.

[50] The ancient commentators take this statute to mean "double in kind" not in value: for example, two cows surrendered for one cow stolen.

[51] That is, neither a thief nor a receiver of stolen goods, whether acquired through purchase or by other method, can acquire title to property in stolen goods through long possession of such.

[52] The uncia (whence our "ounce") is the unit of division of the as and is used also as one-twelfth of anything. One-twelfth of the principal paid yearly as interest equals 8-1/3%.

[53] This originally is a religious penalty, whereby the person is sacrificed. But sacer comes to mean "a person disgraced and outlawed and deprived of his property."

[54] At a sale (*mancipium* or *mancipatio*) the buyer in the presence of five adult citizens had his money weighed by another adult citizen who held scales for this purpose.

This practice obtained originally ere the introduction of coinage.

[55] That is, enactments referring to a single citizen, whether or not in his favor.

[56] Caput includes also privileges of citizenship (*civitas*).

[57] Commonly known as the *comitia centuriata*, an assembly which comprised all citizens. To this assembly a citizen convicted in court on a capital charge had the right of appeal (*ius provocationis*) at least as early as the passage of the Lex Valeria in 509 B.C., for Cicero claims that the pontifical as well as the augural books state that the right of appeal from the regal sentences had been recognized (De Re Publica, 11. 31. 54).

[58] This statute is quoted by Cicero (De Legibus, III. 4. 11), who inserts censores (censors) as the subject of the last verb *locassint* (have placed). But the last clause must have been "modernized" either by Cicero or in his source, because the promulgation of the Twelve Tables in 449 B.C. antedated the creation of the censorship, which can not be traced higher than 443 B.C., if we can believe Livy's account of its institution (op. cit., IV. 8. 2-7). Before that time the consuls superintended the lists of citizens.

[59] The first provision doubtlessly descends from a primitive tribal tabu. Cicero supposes that the second provision is due to danger from fire (De Legibus, II. 23. 58).

[60] In view of the simplicity enjoined in some of the following statutes of this Table, for the decemvirs apparently took a dim view of extravagant funerals, this statute seems to mean that a rough-hewn pyre without elaborate smoothness of its wooden material suffices for the cremation-couch of a citizen.

[61] Cicero says that some older interpreters suspected that some kind of mourning-garment was meant by *lessus*, but that he inclines to the interpretation that it signifies a sort of sorrowful wailing (De Legibus, II.23.59)

[62] This provision is aimed at the common custom of prolonging mourning by gathering and preserving unburied some part of the corpse. When this part (*os resectum*) later had been buried, then only mourning ceased. It is possible that some Romans may have thought that cremation might be wrong or that its ceremony was inadequate.

[63] That is, in such a case a limb could be carried to Rome and then buried.

[64] That is, a garland or a chaplet or a wreath as a prize of achievement.

[65] A chattel, for example, is a slave or a horse who wins a wreath for the owner.

[66] Cicero says that this statute seems to suggest fear of disastrous fire (*De Legibus*, II. 24. 61).

[67] In the burning-mound also ashes were buried.

[68] This statute proved so unpopular that it soon was repealed by the Lex Canuleia in 445 B.C.

[69] This process of "taking a pledge" is the seizure and the detention of a debtor's property or part thereof to induce the debtor to pay the debt before any other legal action will be taken.

It will be noticed that the two instances given in this statute concern Sacred Law, with which by anticipation the fourth statute of this Table likewise is concerned. Modern scholars place these two provisions among the Supplementary Laws despite the temptation to set these among the statutes of Table X, of which all but one item come from Cicero's discussion of Sacred Law in his *De Legibus*, II. 23. 58-24. 61, in the concluding portion of which Cicero seems to speak with some finality that he has given all the regulations regarding religion found in the Twelve Tables. Moreover these two rules come from Gaius, who flourished more than two centuries after Cicero. But if every Supplementary Law resembling the subject-matter of Tables I-X should be advanced to the appropriate position forward, few would be the statutes left in Tables XI-XII. It is merely coincidental that some of the statutes among the Supplementary Laws should concern topics already treated, for from the Romans we must not remove the faculty of aftersight.

[70] Some scholars seek to place this provision in Table VIII, where it seems properly to belong, despite its traditional position here.

This dislocation, coupled with that of the preceding provision, well illustrates how hopeless is our reconstruction of the order of the regulations of the Twelve Tables.

[71] That is, apparently, if a person with or without fraudulent intent had held and claimed as his a thing which a judicial court now decided belonged to another party.

[72] Retention of the article is deemed to have brought the defendant some profit; therefore he must pay double this profit.

[73] Cf. second paragraph in note [69] *supra*.

[74] That is, the most recent law repeals all previous laws which are inconsistent with it.

[75] Cicero says that many laws in the Twelve Tables exhibit this rule (*De Re Publica*, II. 31. 54).

Milton Keynes UK
Ingram Content Group UK Ltd.
UKHW020825231024
450026UK00004B/394